MANDALA COLORING

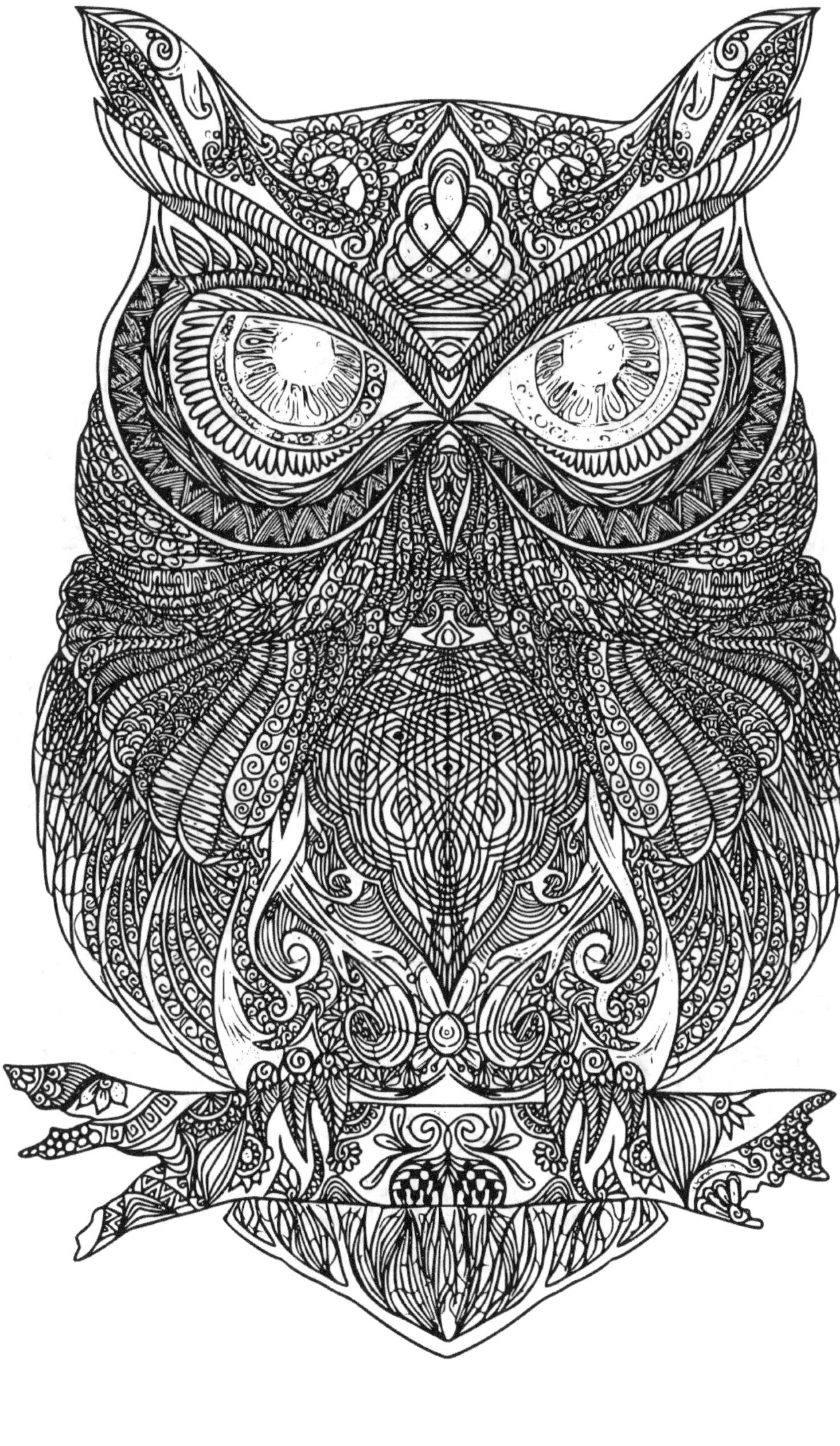

MANDALA COLORING

MANDALA COLORING

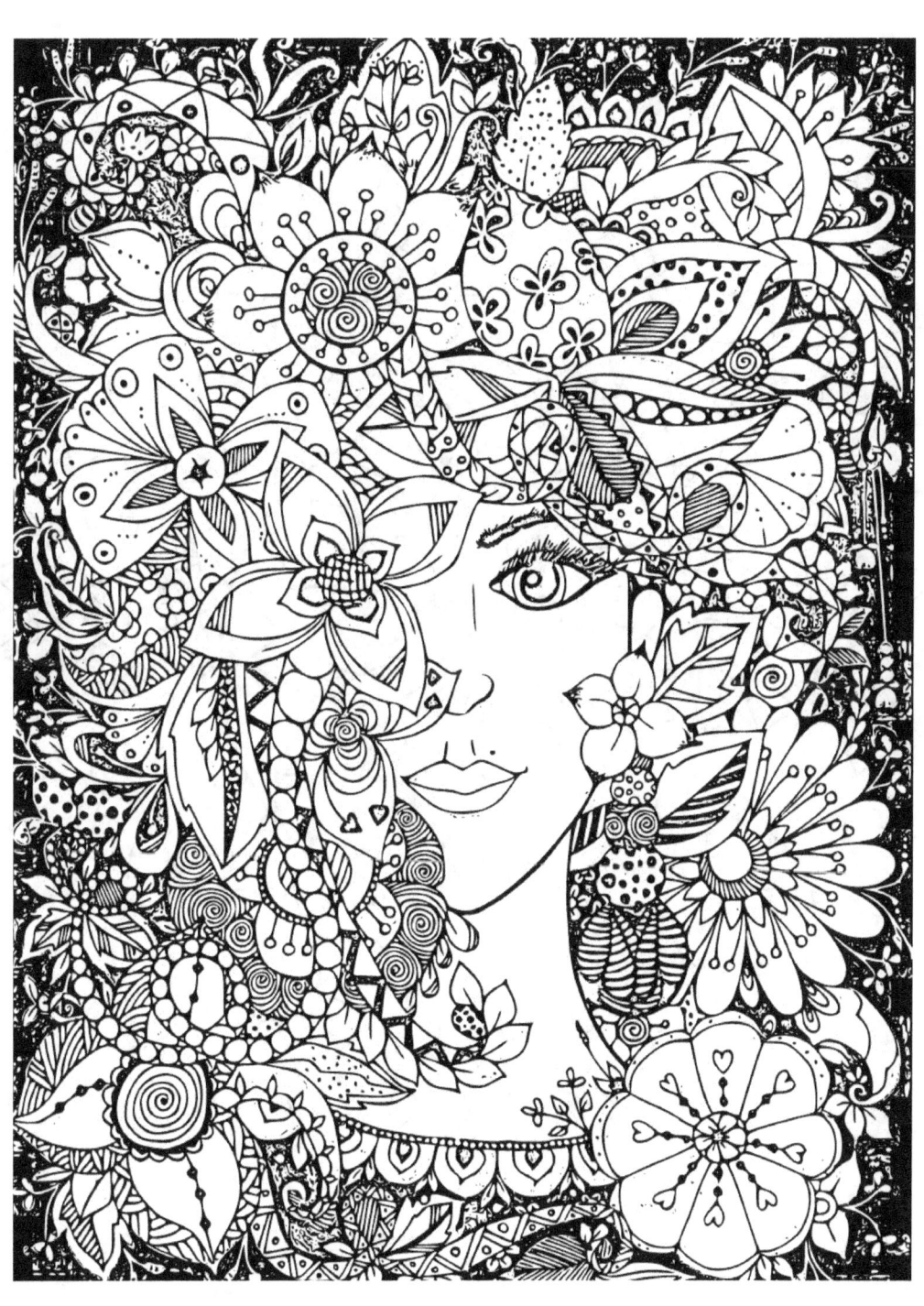

MANDALA COLORING

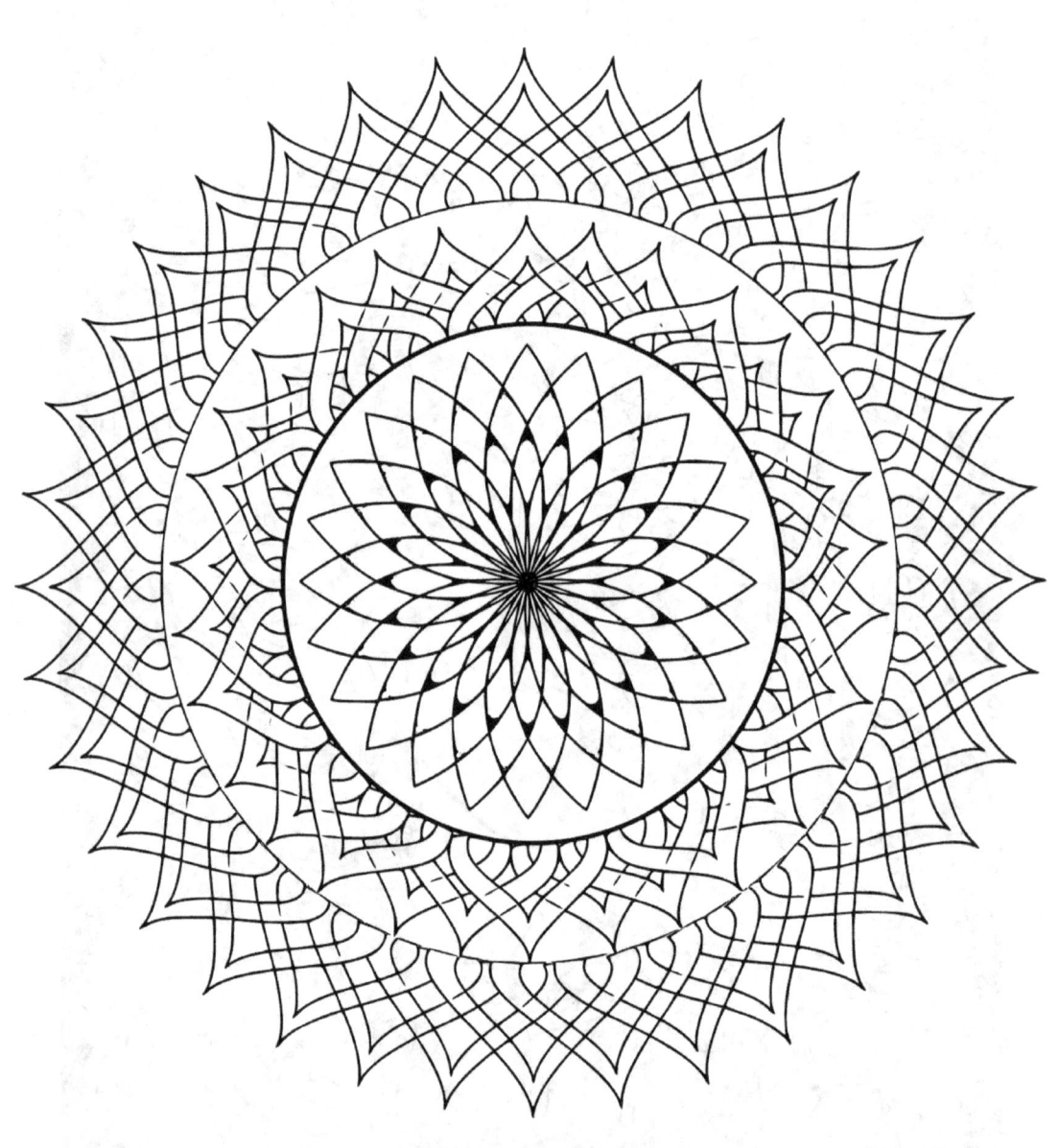

MANDALA COLORING

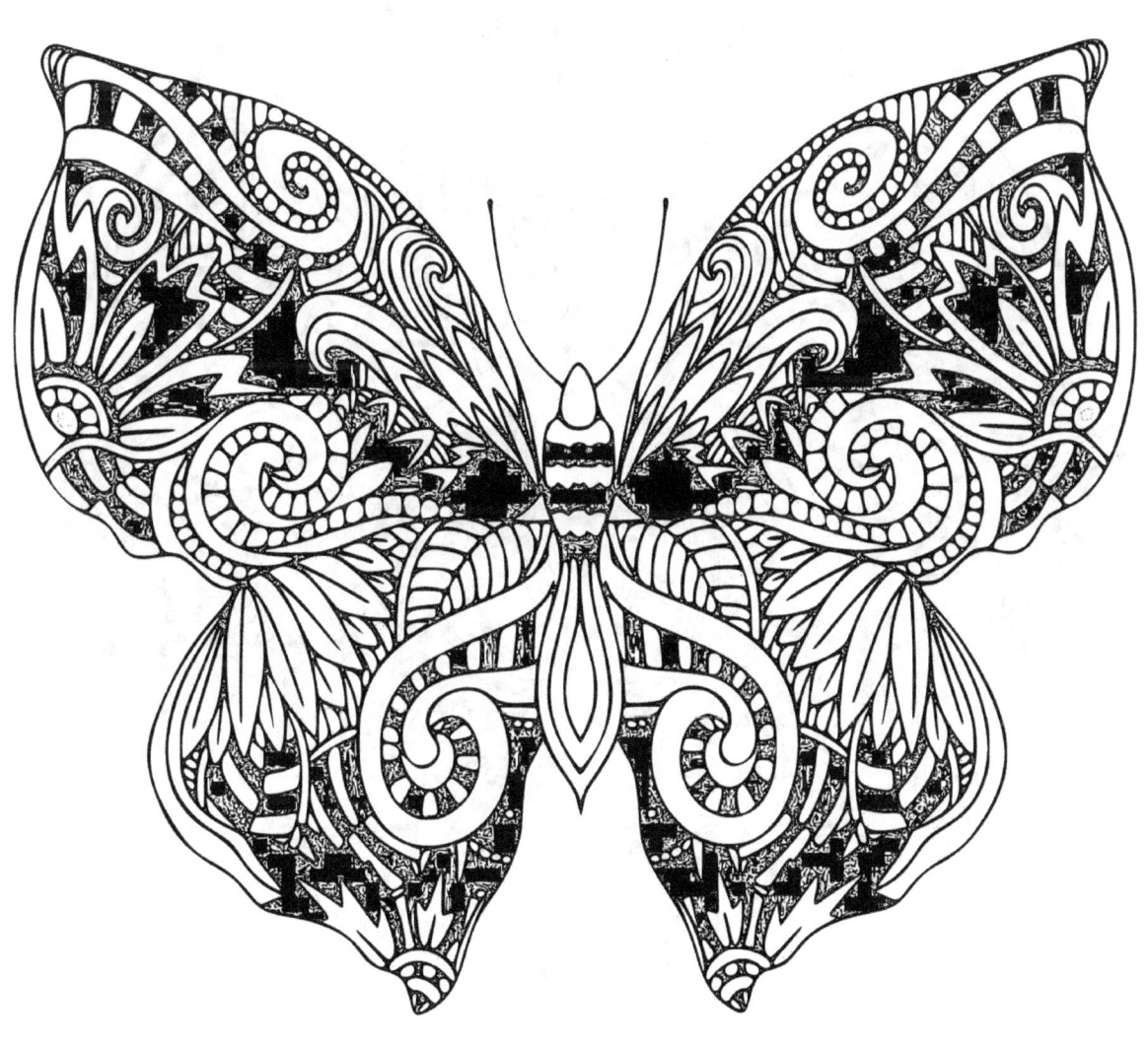

MANDALA COLORING

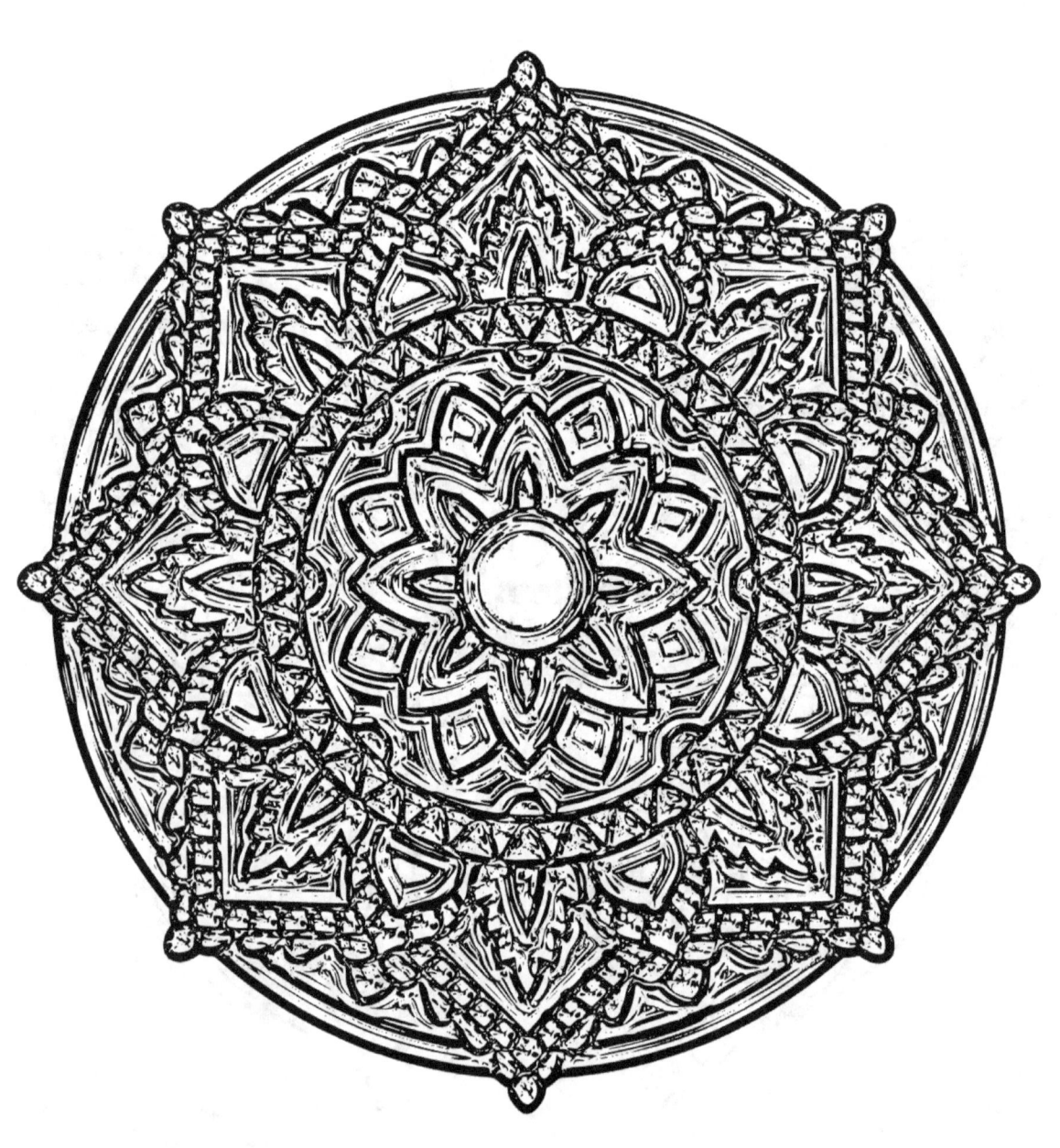

MANDALA COLORING

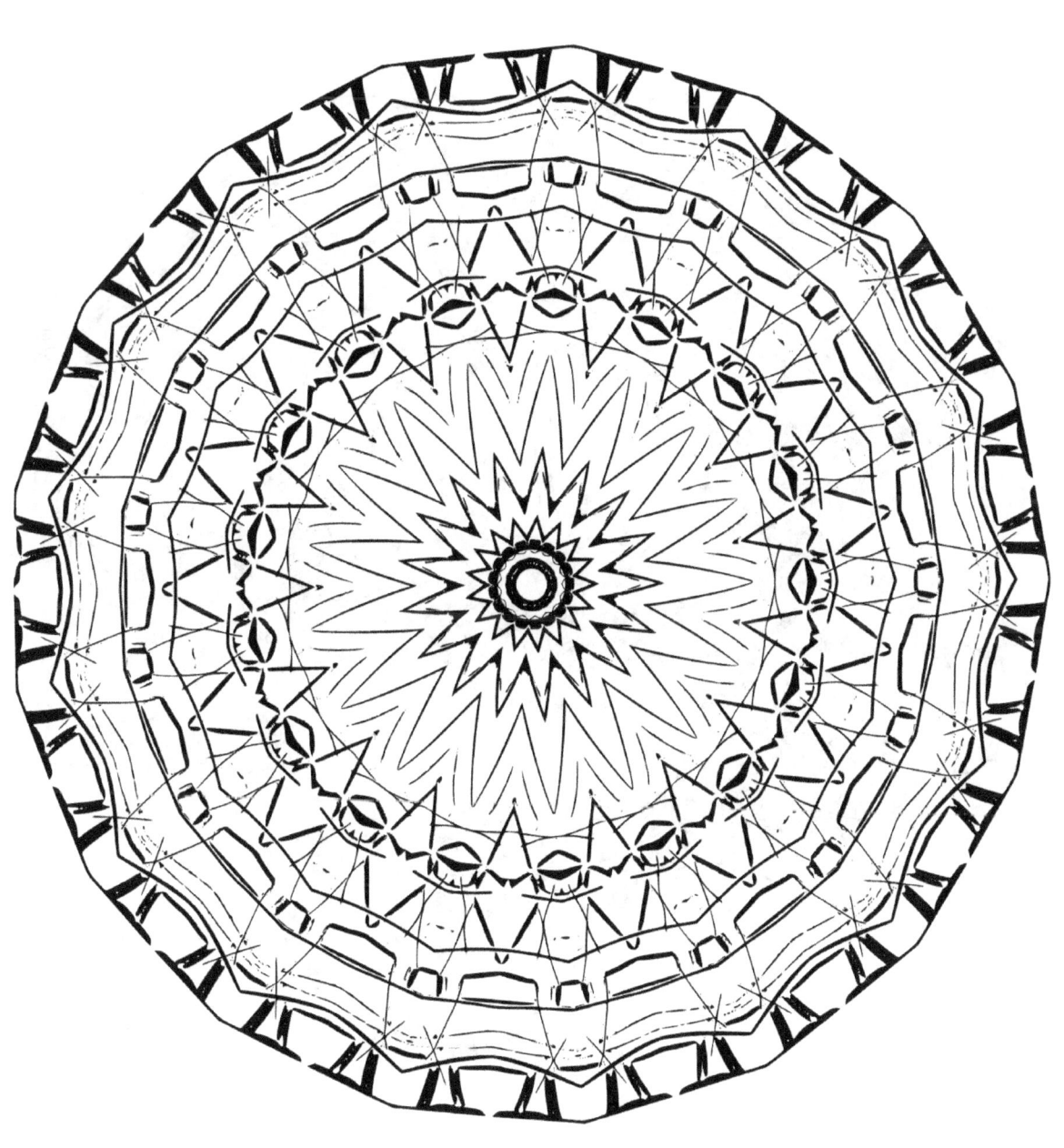

MANDALA COLORING

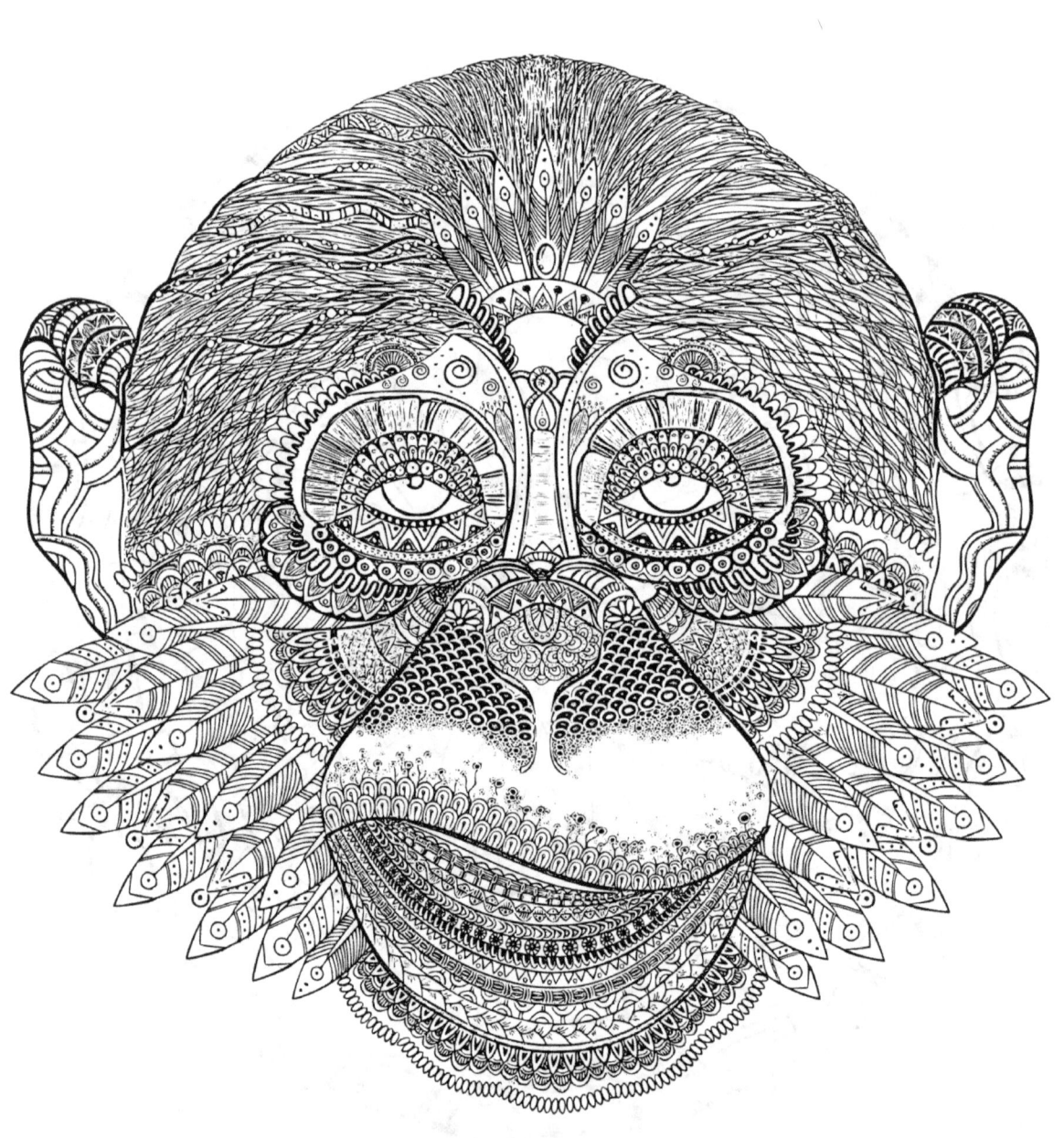

MANDALA COLORING

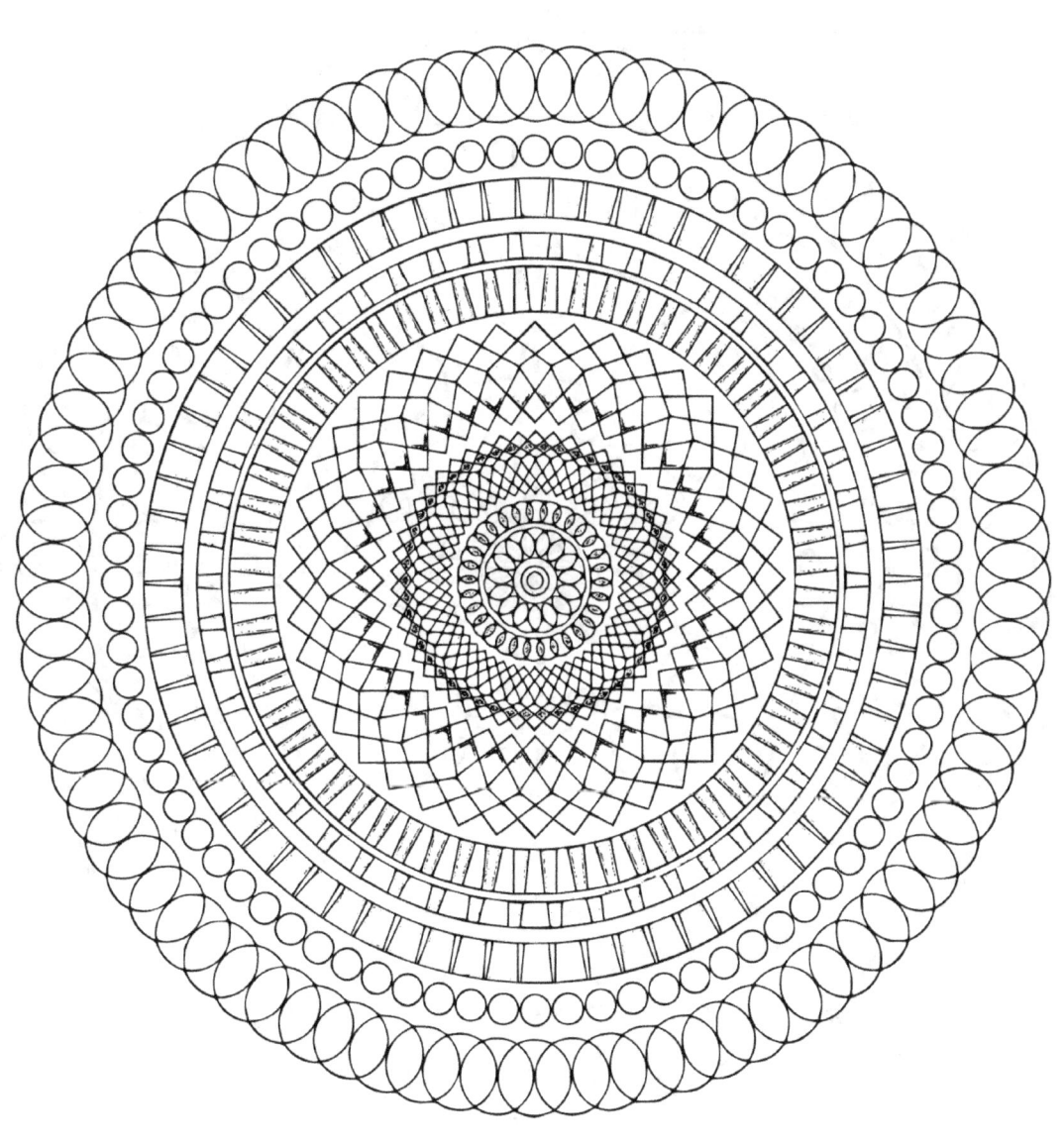

MANDALA COLORING

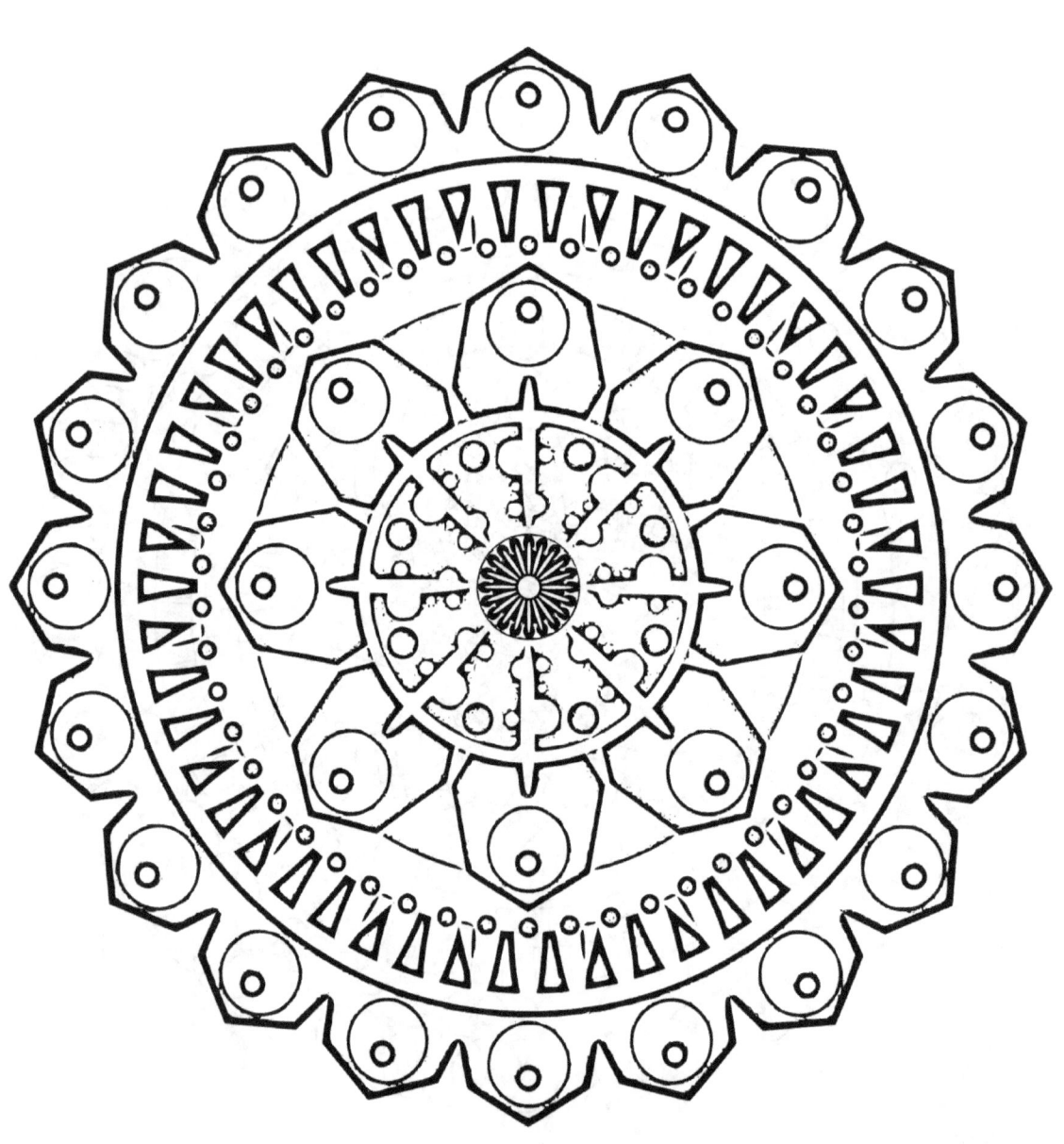

MANDALA COLORING

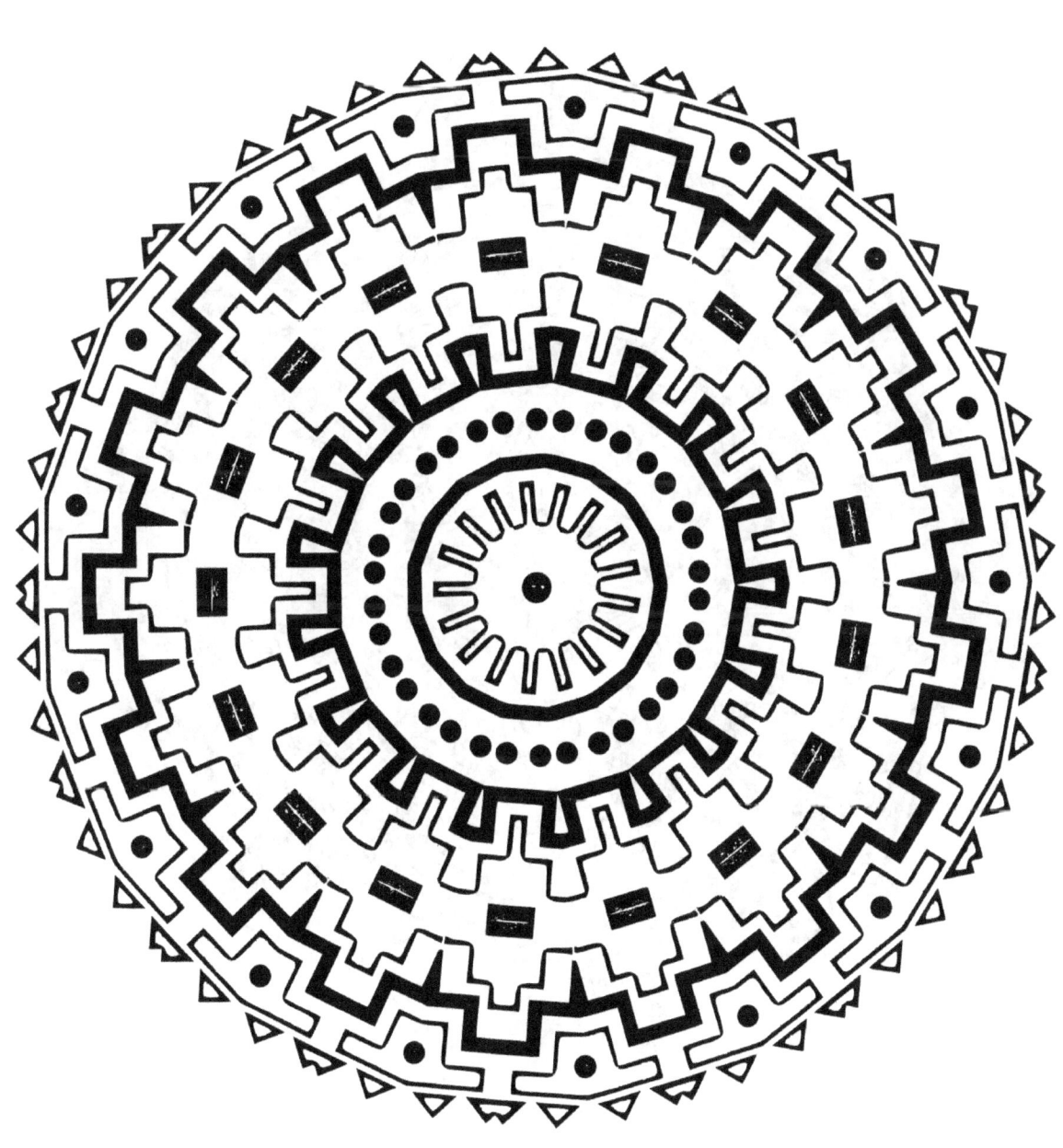

MANDALA COLORING

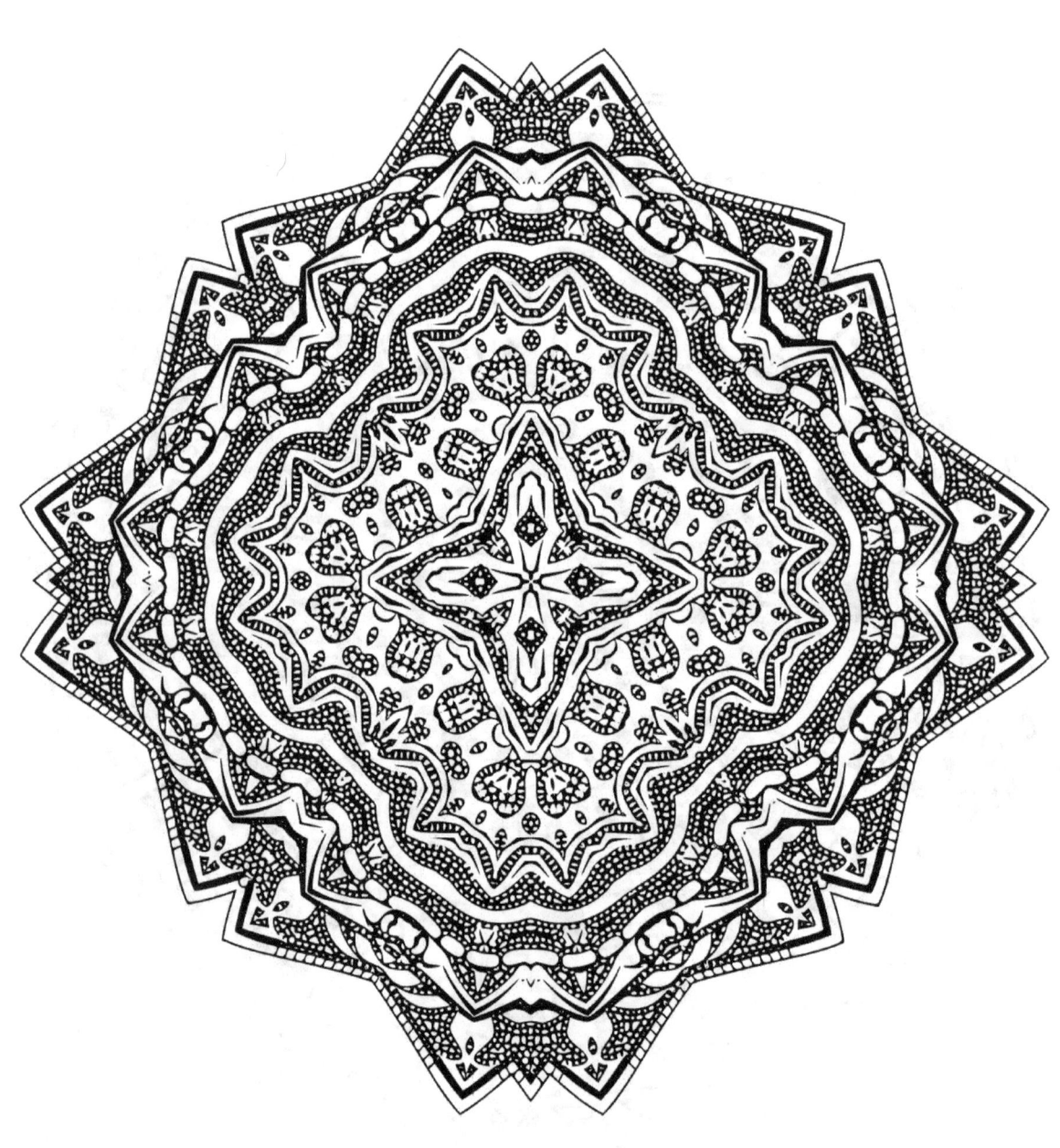

MANDALA COLORING

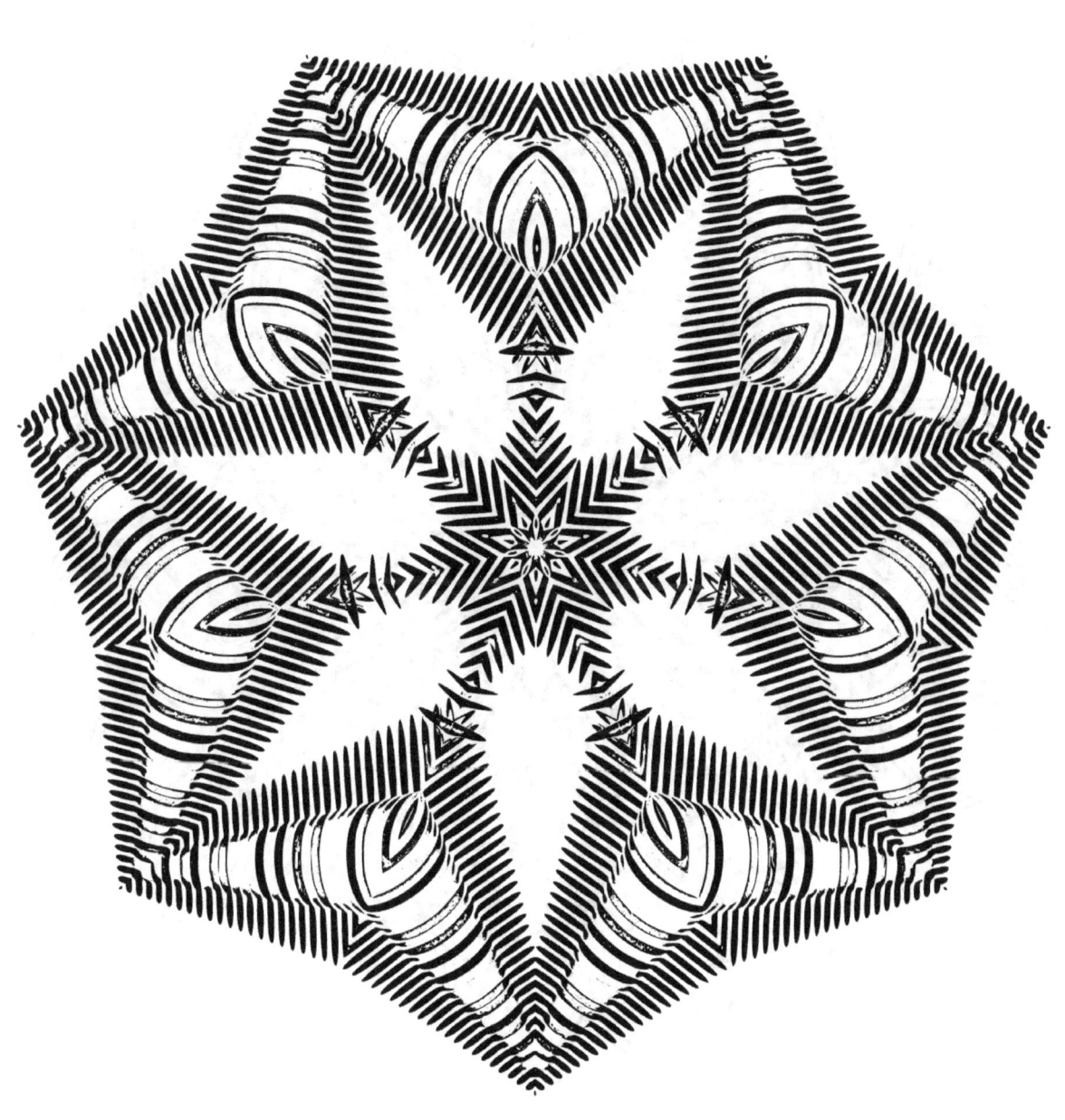

MANDALA COLORING

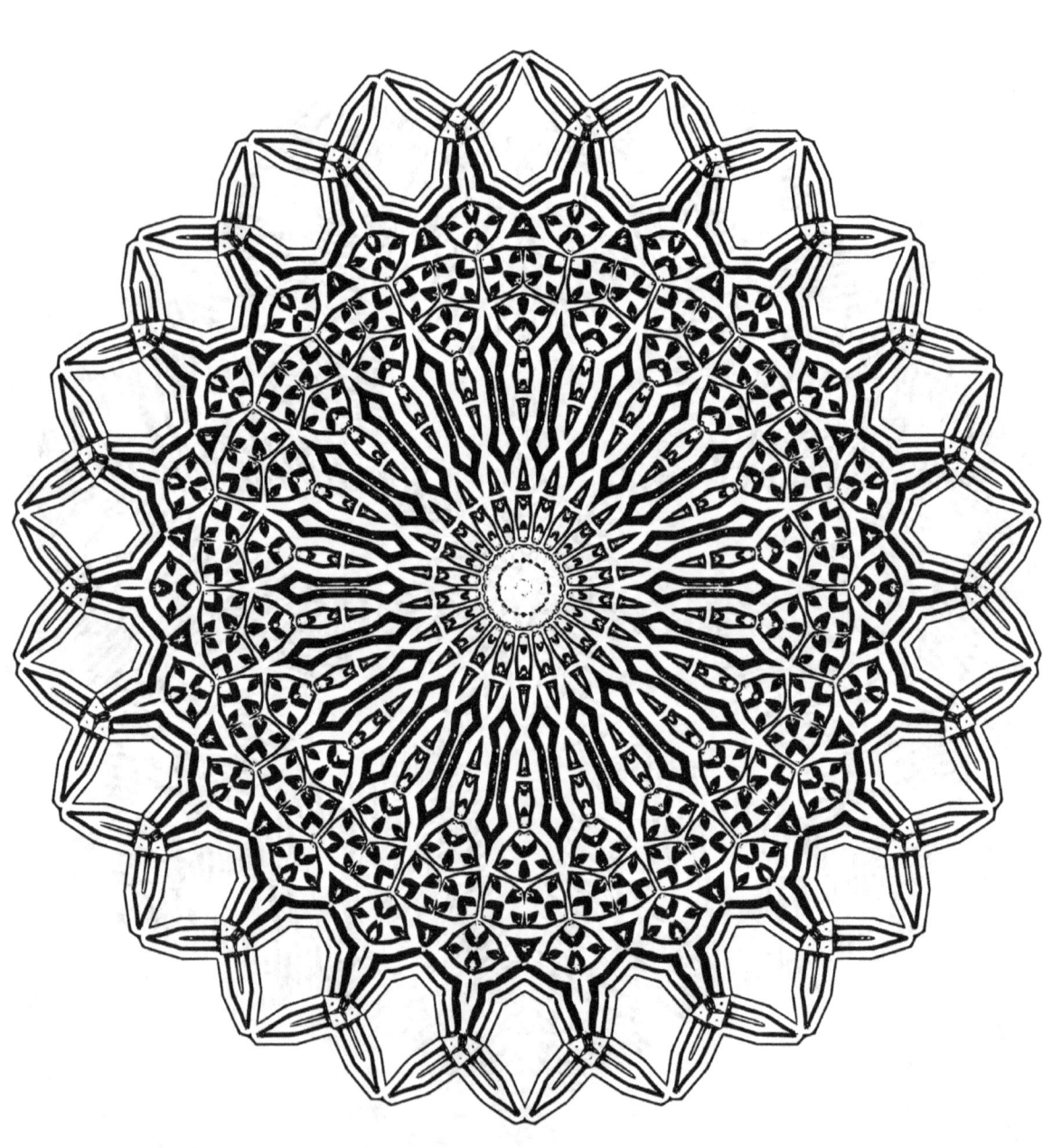

MANDALA COLORING

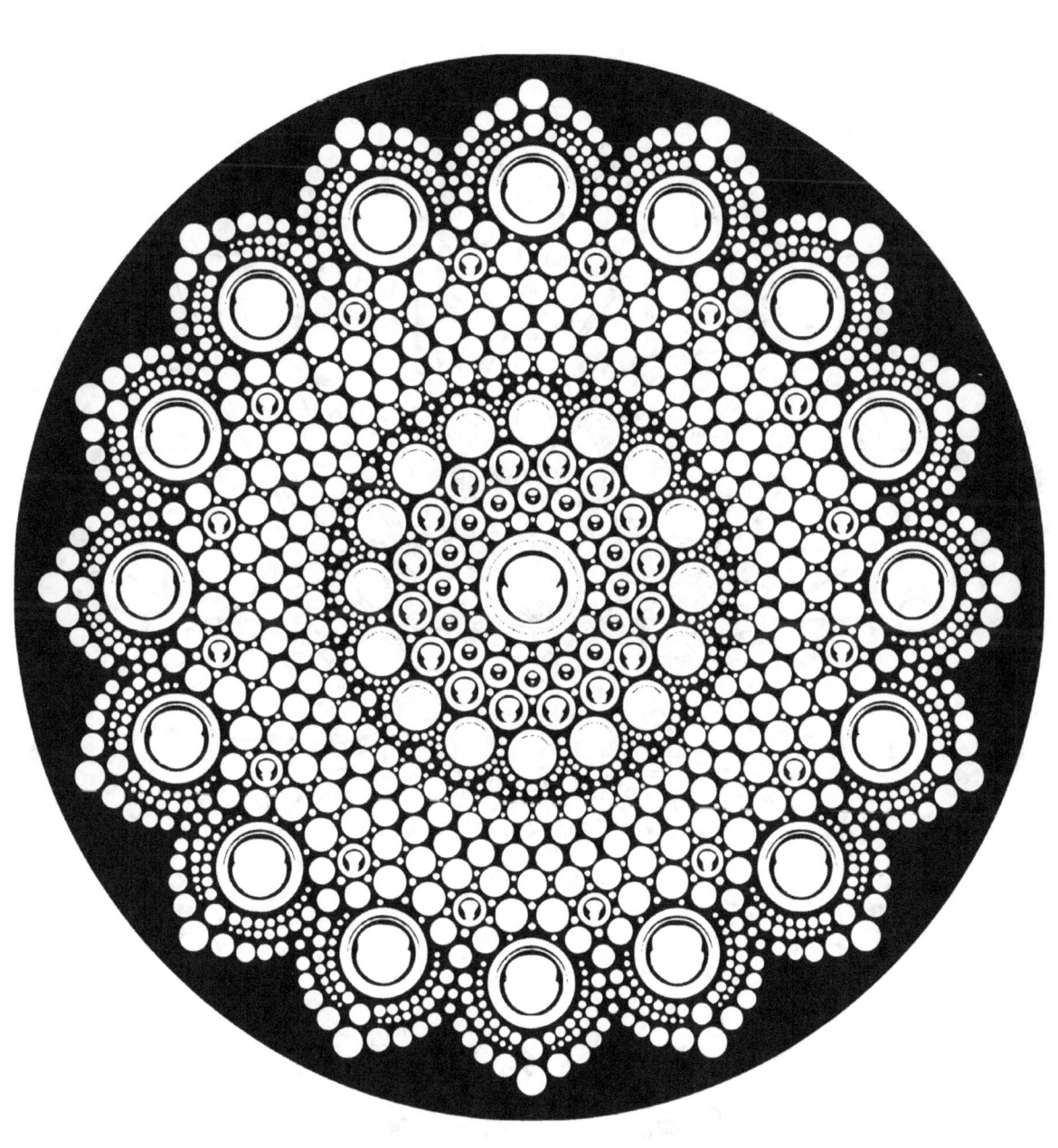

MANDALA COLORING

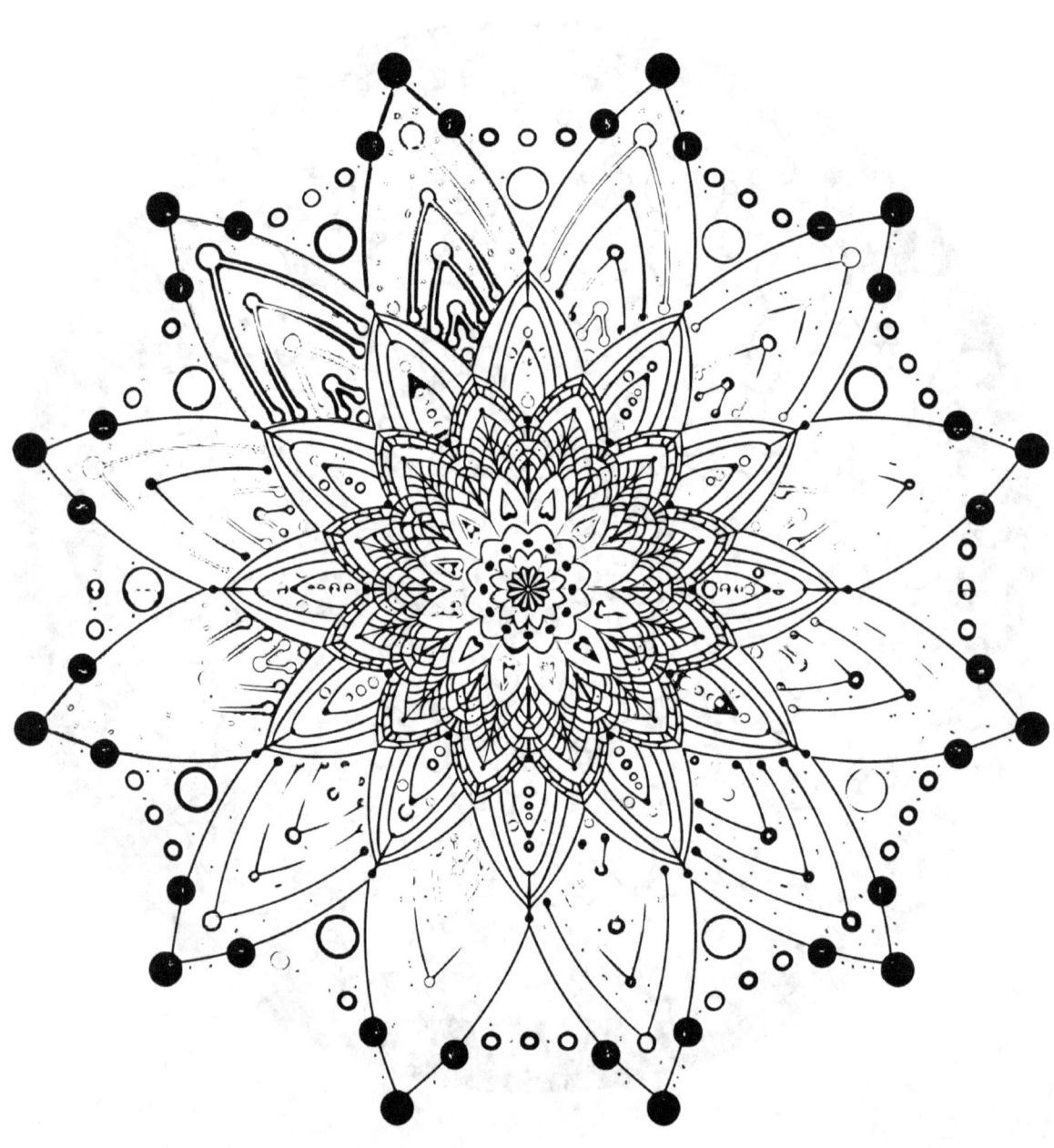

MANDALA COLORING

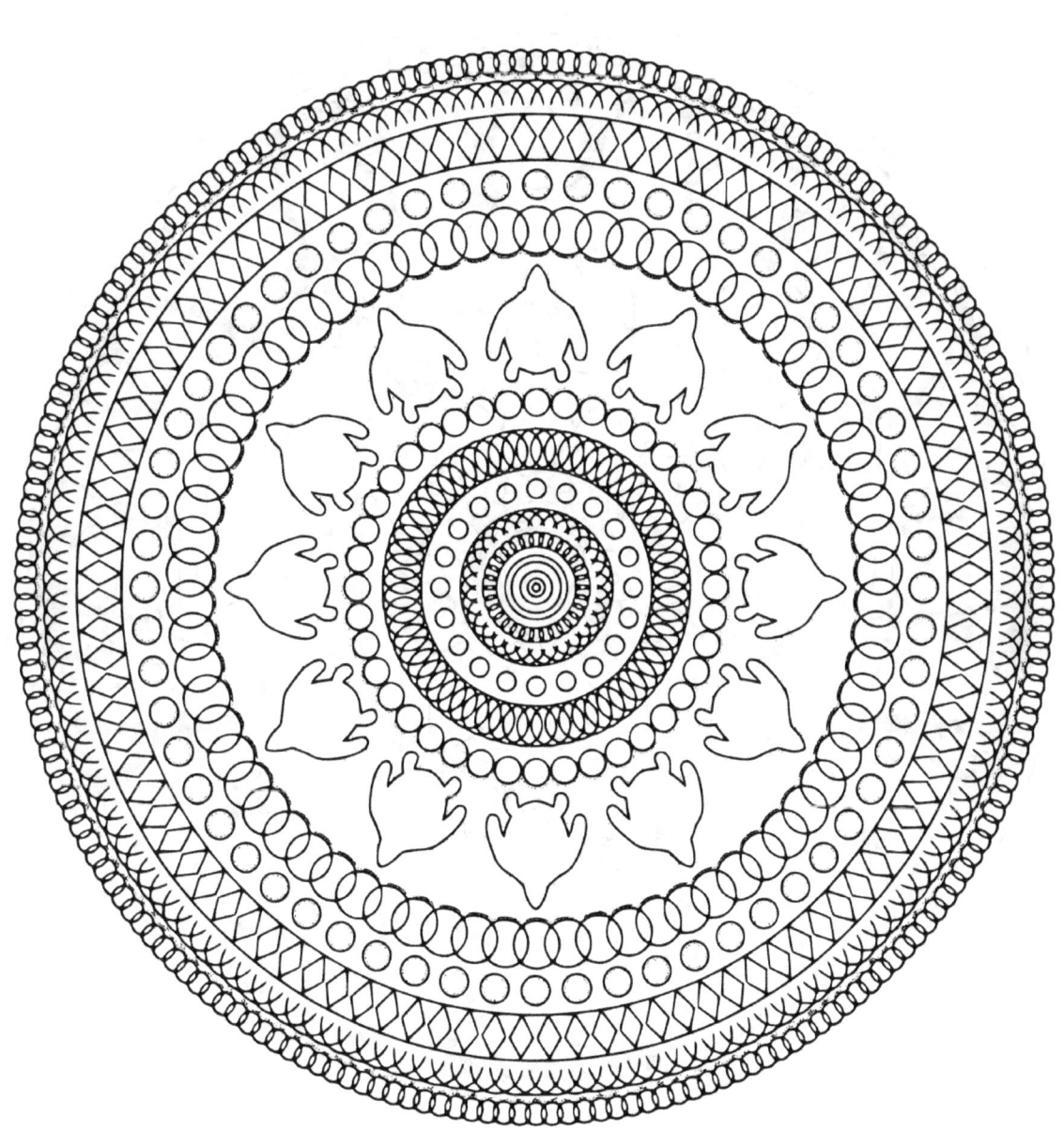

MANDALA COLORING

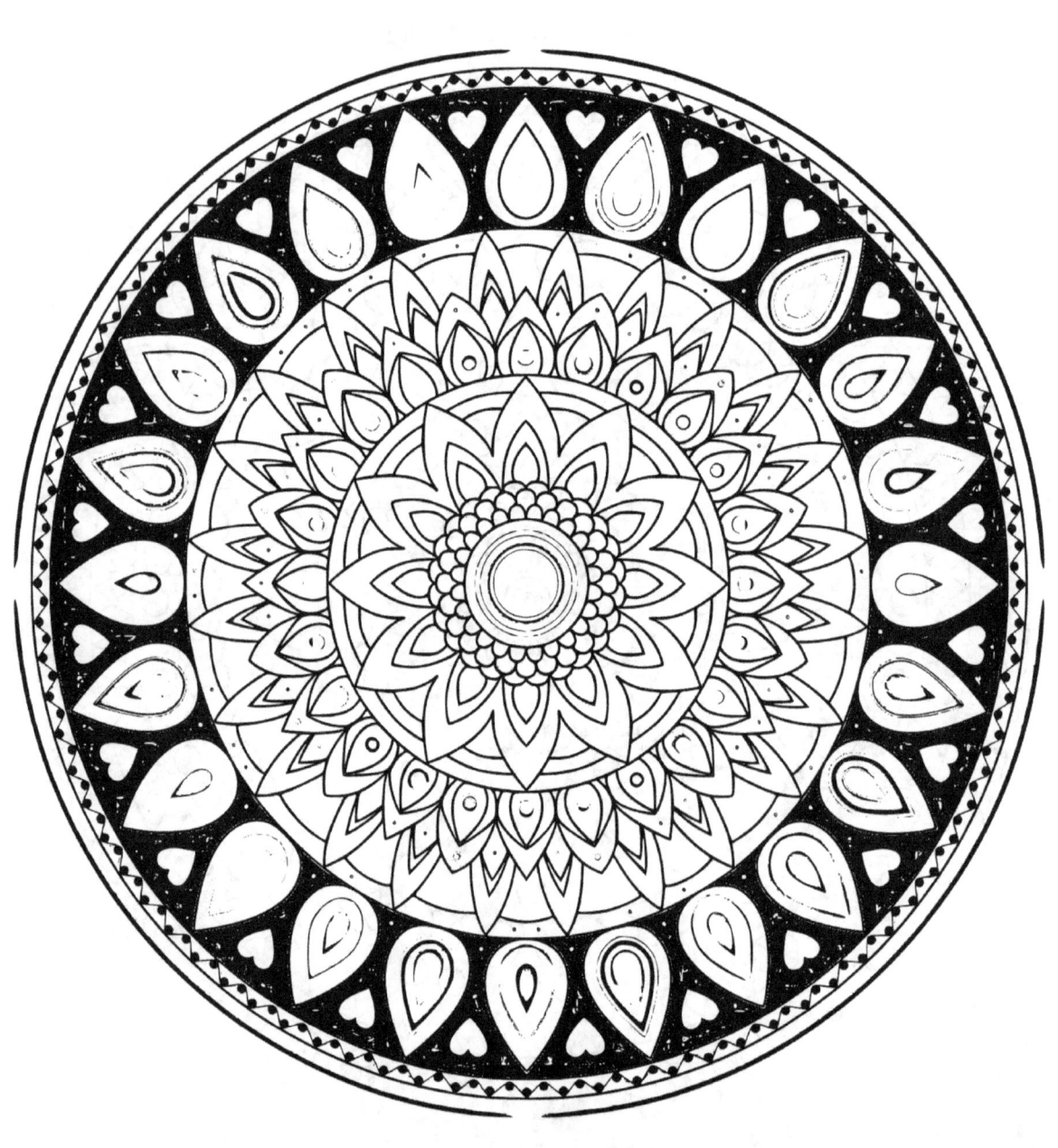

MANDALA COLORING

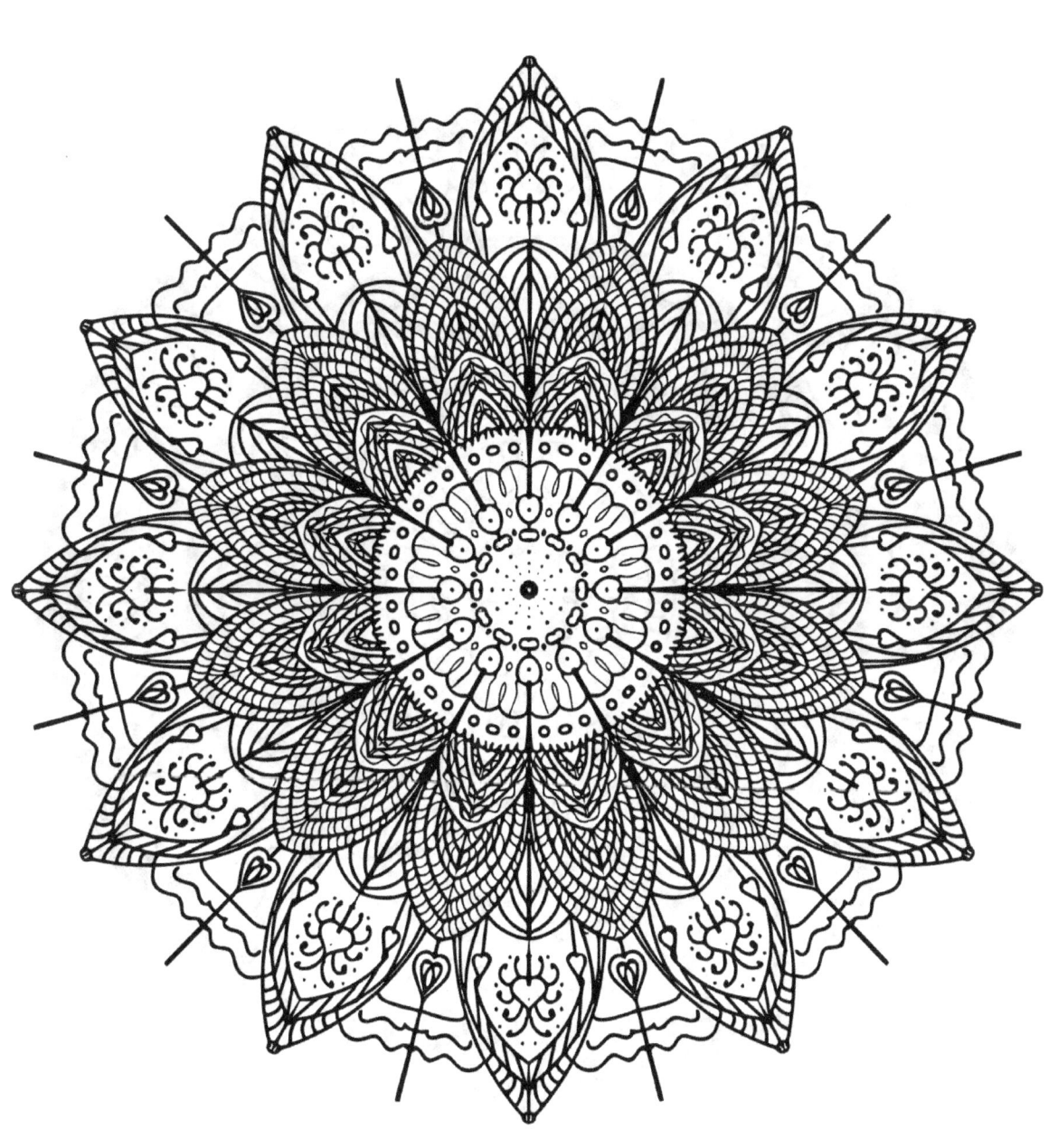

MANDALA COLORING

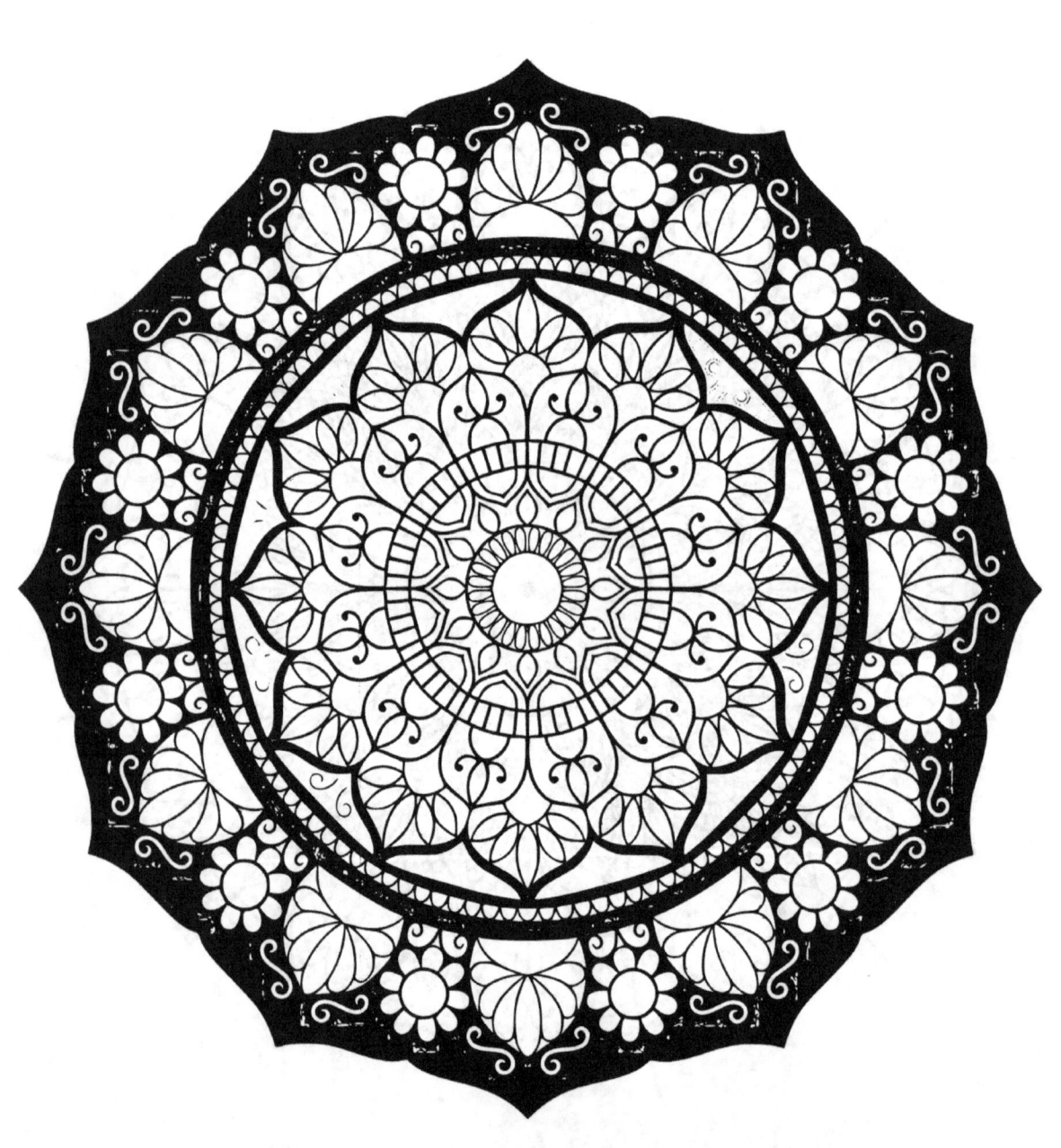

MANDALA COLORING

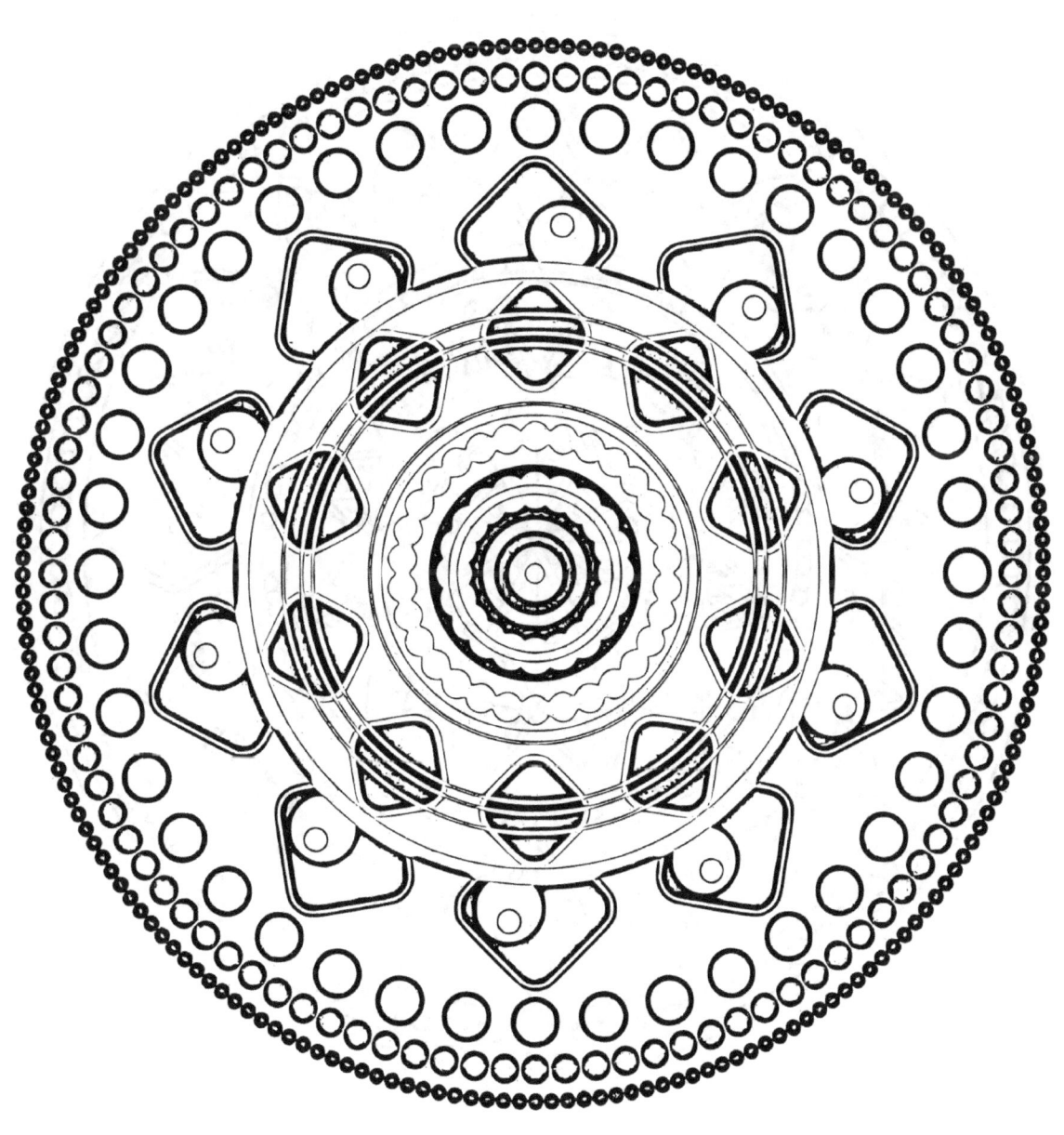

MANDALA COLORING

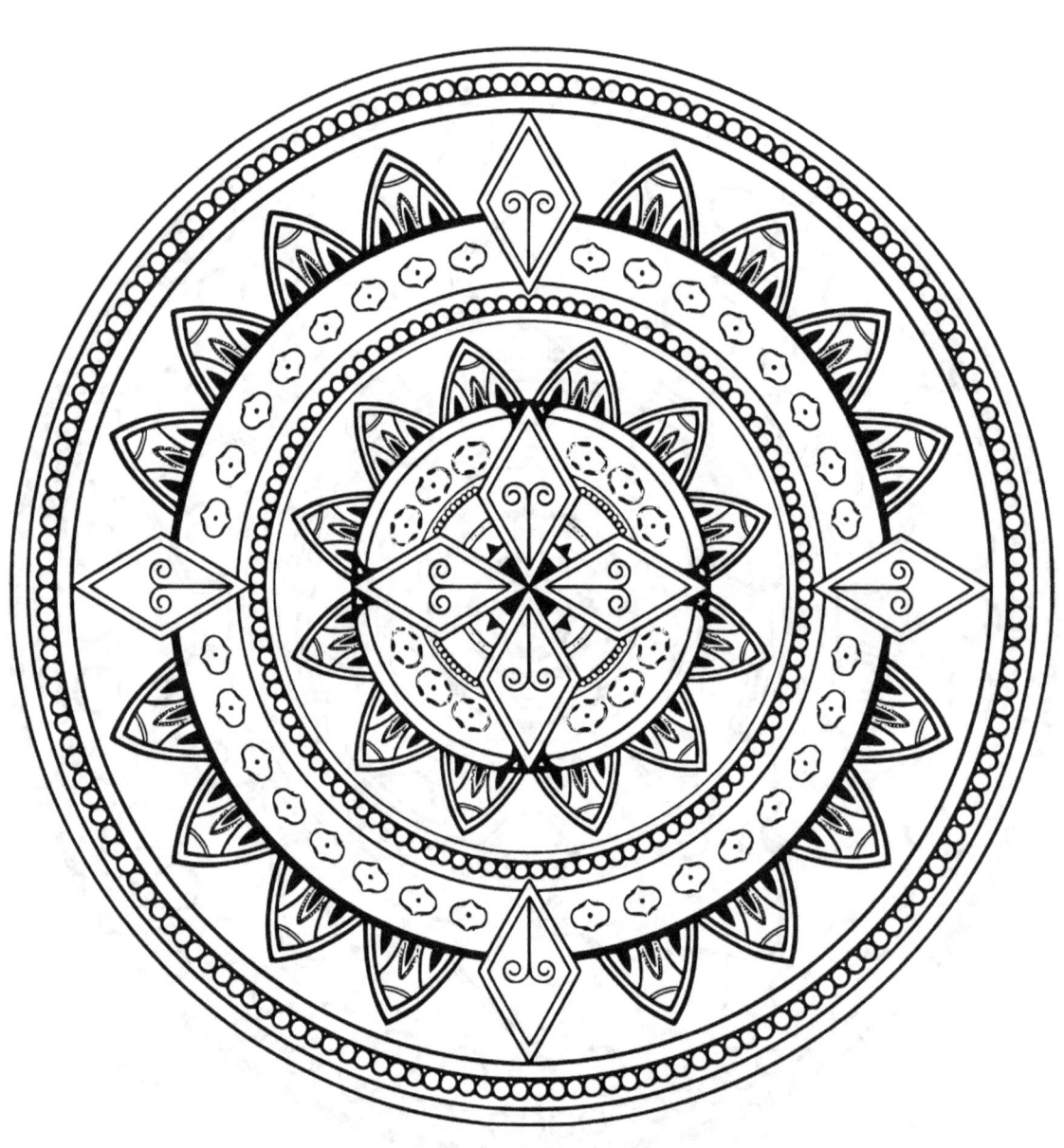

MANDALA COLORING

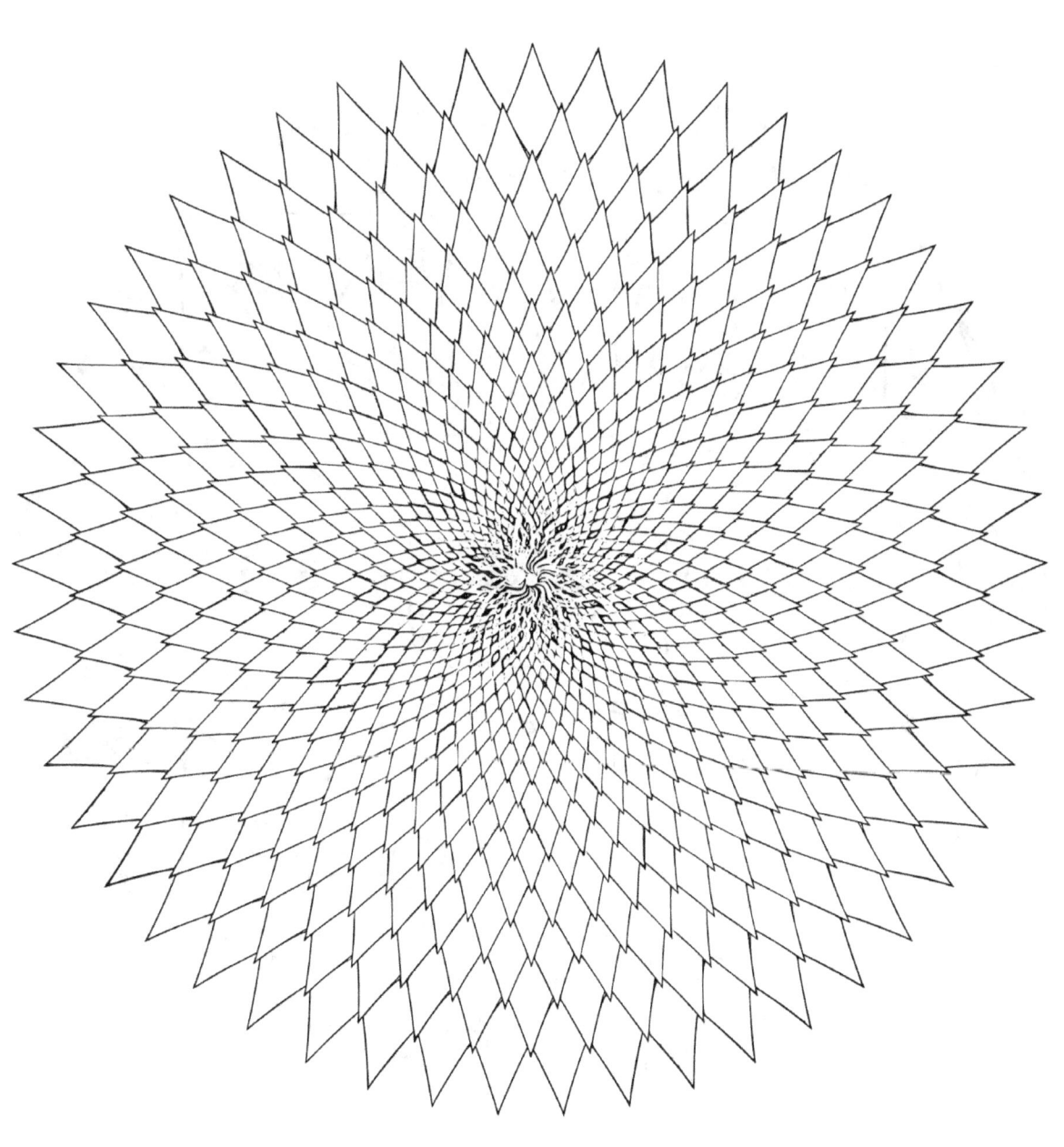

MANDALA COLORING

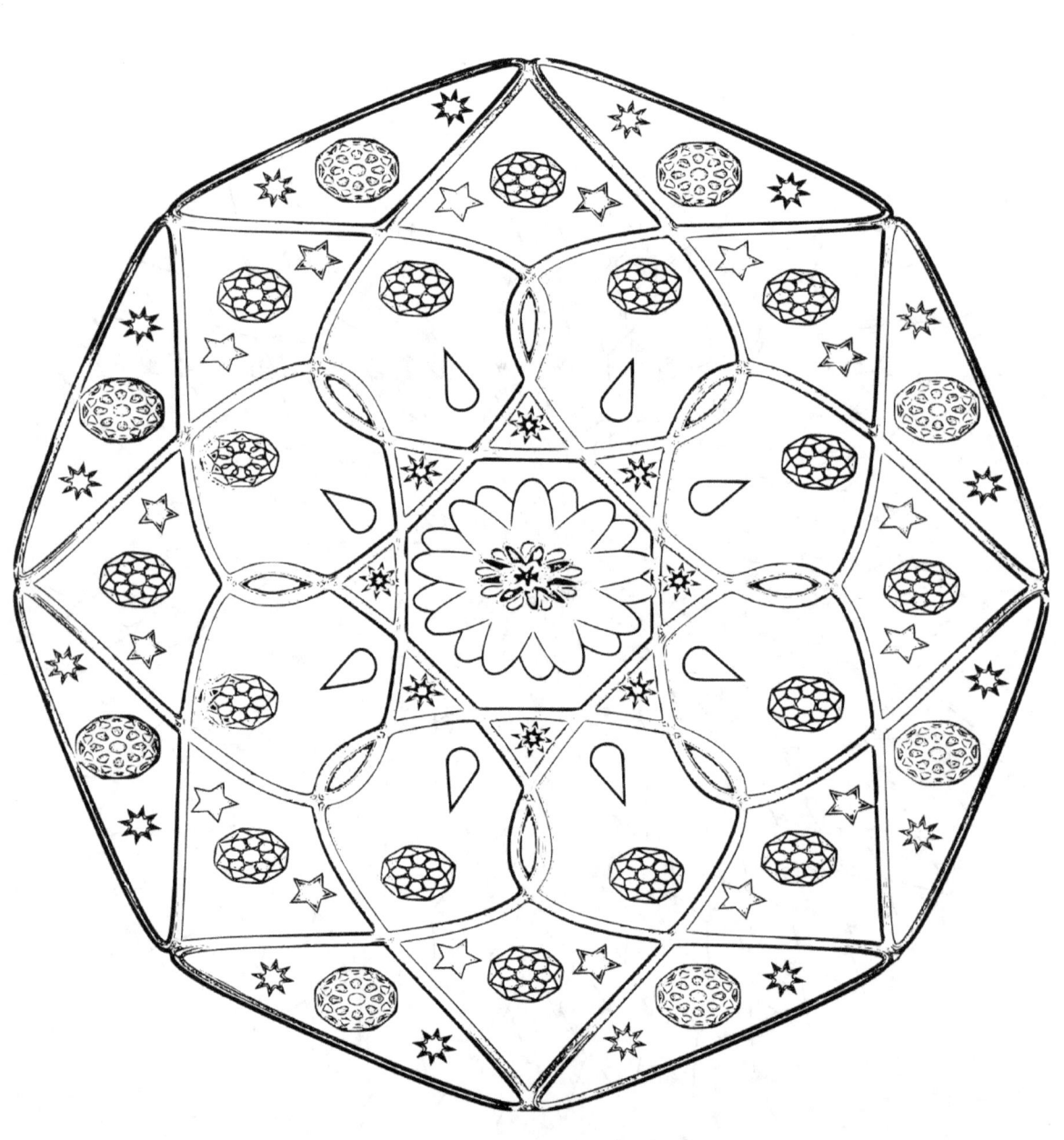

MANDALA COLORING

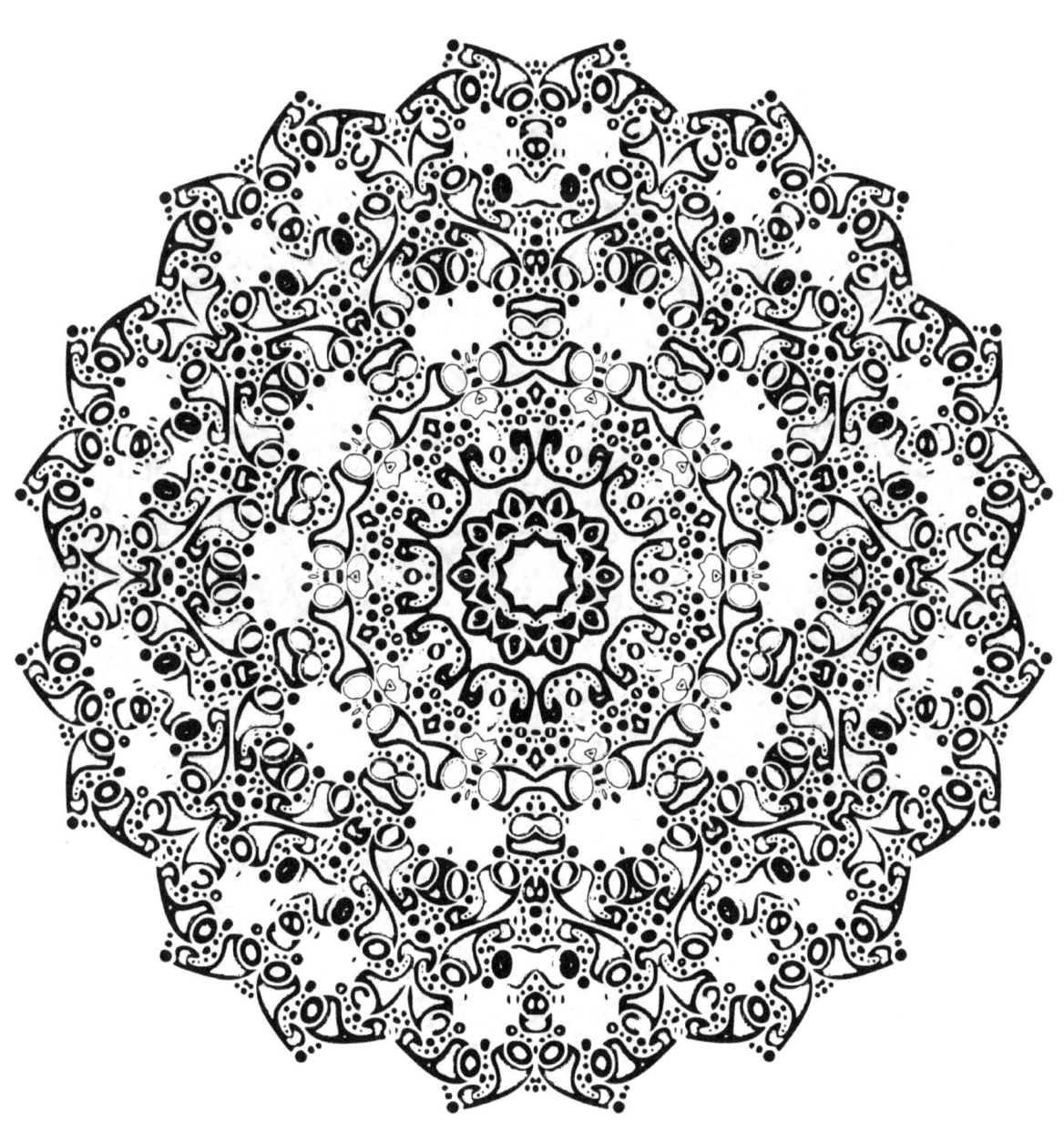

MANDALA COLORING

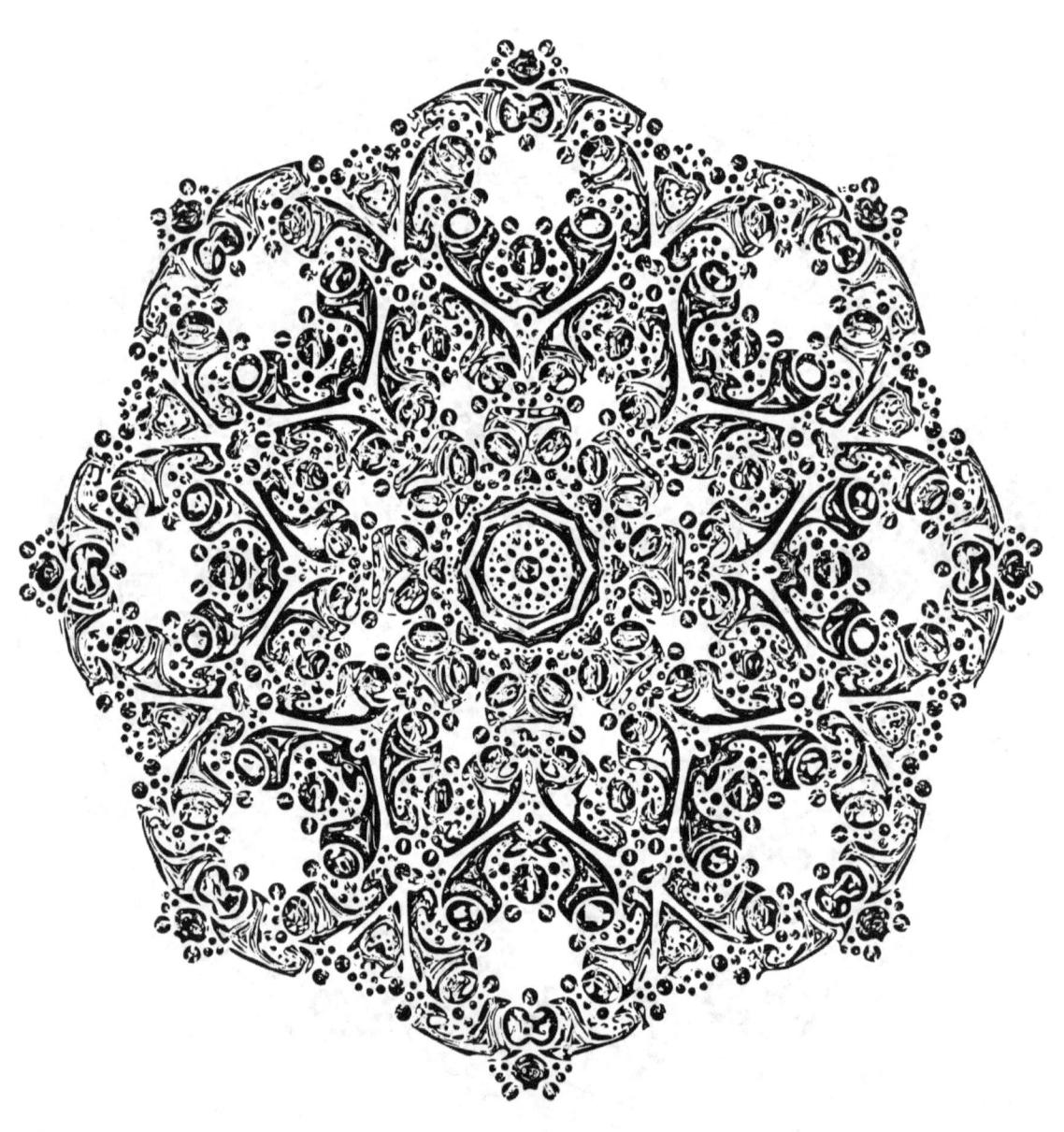

MANDALA COLORING

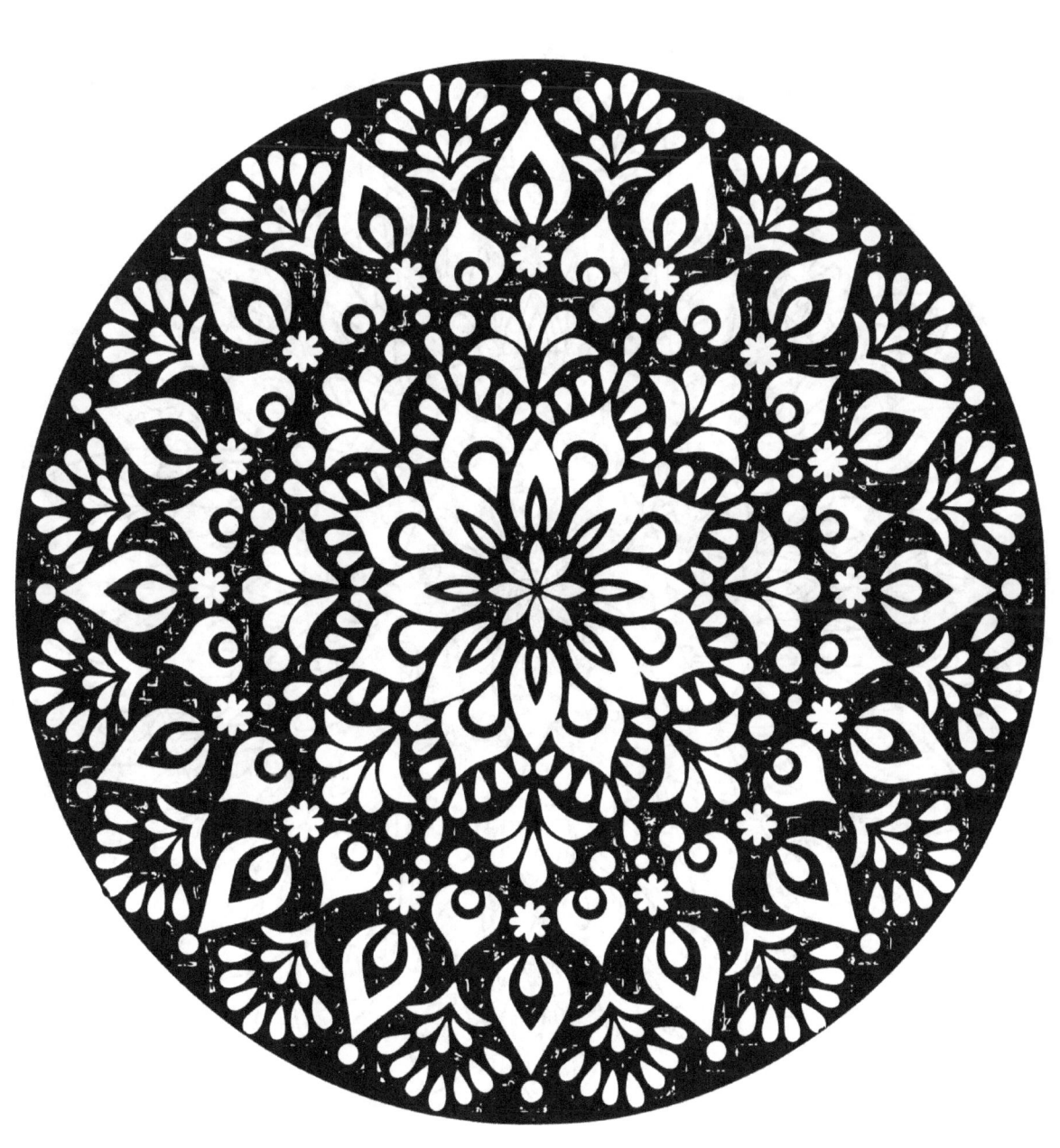

MANDALA COLORING

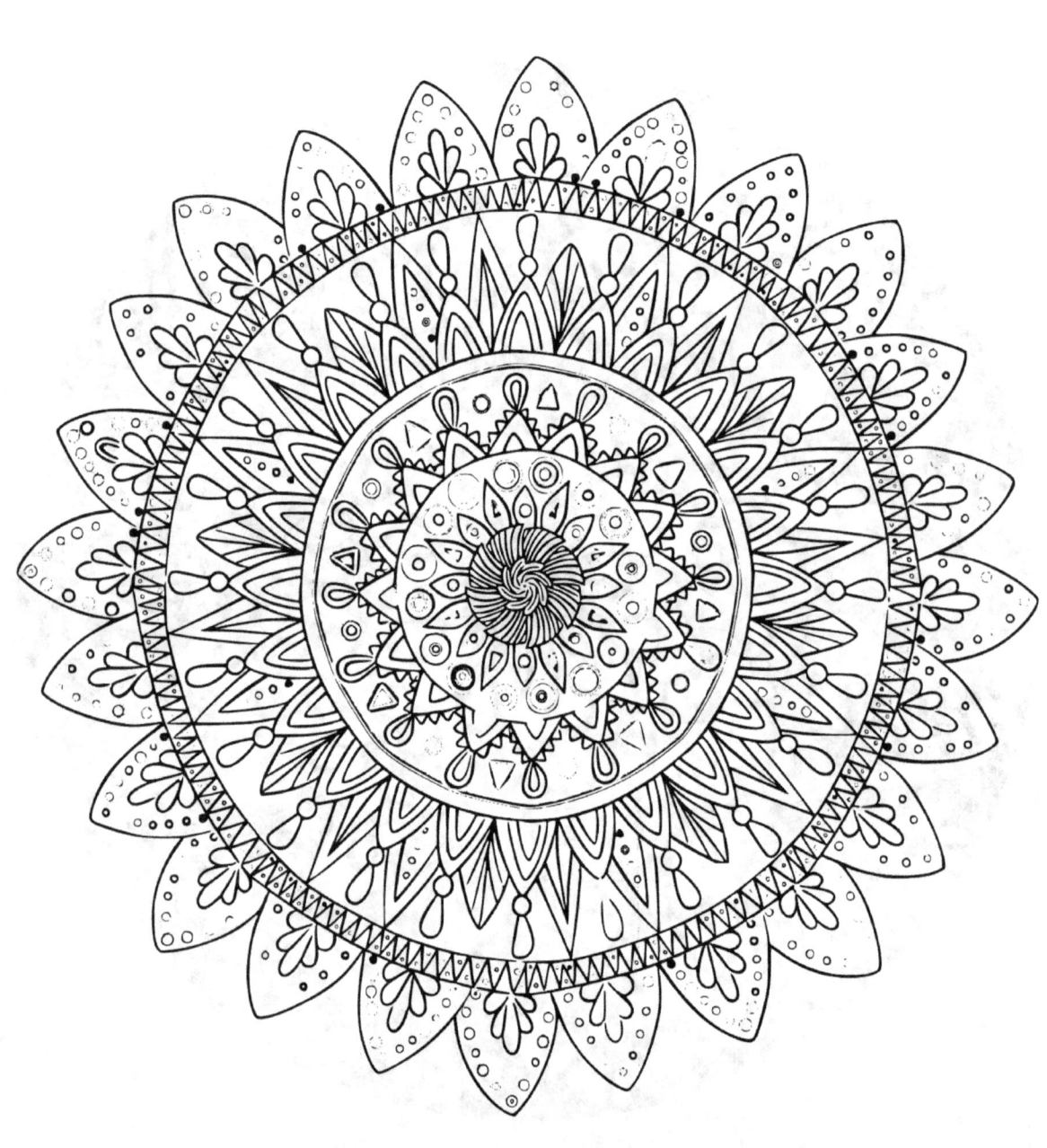

MANDALA COLORING

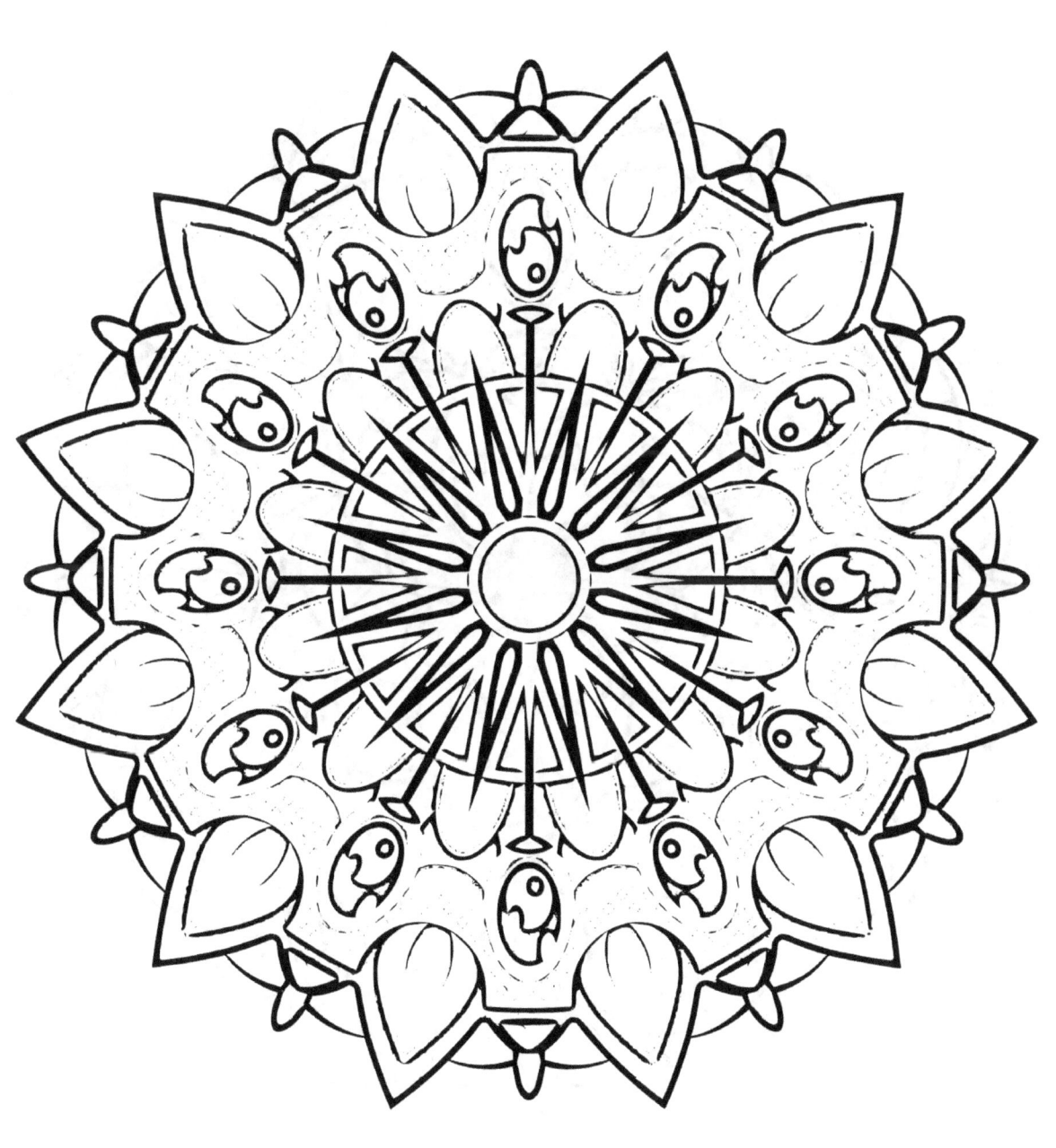

MANDALA COLORING

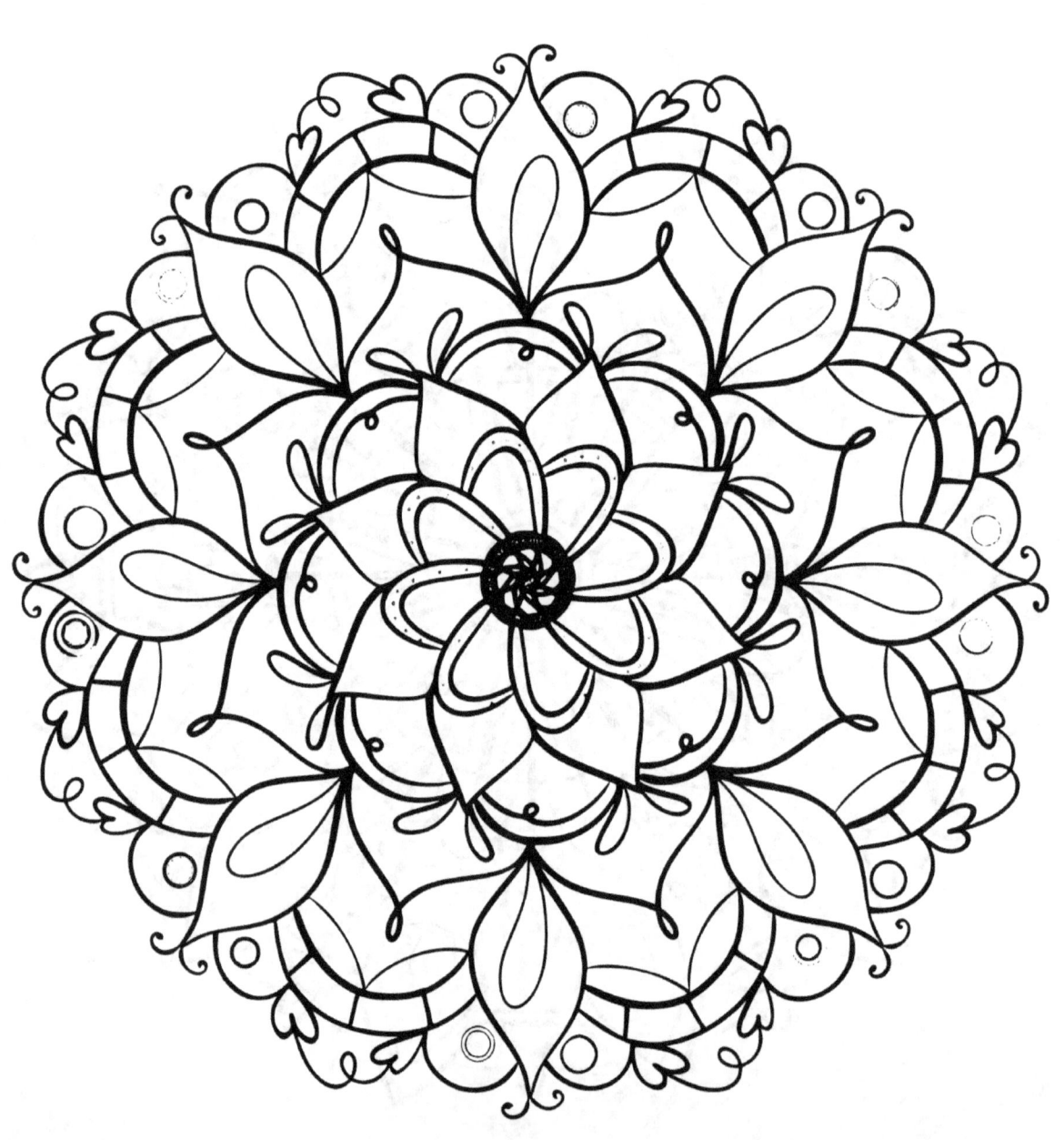